INDIAN COUNTRY STYLEBOOK

For editors, writers and journalists

*With briefings on American Indian Law
and News Gathering in Indian Country*

WASHINGTON STATE EDITION 2017–18

KITSAP
PUBLISHING

Indian Country Stylebook
Washington State Edition 2017–18

Second edition, published 2017

By Richard Walker, Jackie Jacobs,
Gabriel Galanda and Louie Gong

Copyright © 2017, Richard Walker, Jackie Jacobs,
Gabriel Galanda and Louie Gong

Cover art by Louie Gong

ISBN 978-1-942661-68-9

Published by Kitsap Publishing
P.O. Box 1269
Poulsbo, WA 98370
www.KitsapPublishing.com

Printed in the United States of America

TD 20170612

20-10 9 8 7 6 5 4 3 2 1

INDIAN COUNTRY STYLEBOOK
2017–18 EDITION

Fully reviewed guide containing:

- More than 100 entries.
- Briefing on American Indian Law.
- Briefing on news gathering in Indian Country.
- Directory of indigenous nations and leaders in Washington State.
- Directory of Indian Country media in Washington state.

ACKNOWLEDGMENTS

The following individuals participated in the creation of this stylebook: Richard Walker, Mexican/Yaqui, style guide and directories; Gabriel Galanda, Round Valley, and Amber Penn-Roco, Chehalis, "Briefing on American Indian Law"; Jackie Jacobs, Lumbee, "Briefing on News Gathering in Indian Country"; Louie Gong, Nooksack, cover art.

The authors thank the following professionals for their generosity of time and expertise in reviewing this guide prior to publication: Darrell Hillaire, Lummi; Sen. John McCoy, Tulalip Tribes; Steve Robinson, Salish-Kootenai descent; Mark Trahant, Shoshone-Bannock; Michael Vendiola, Swinomish.

The authors thank the Potlatch Fund and the Samish Nation for their generosity of resources and time in making this edition more available.

ABOUT THE COVER

"The 'Eagle Vision' design features a Coast Salish eagle — which is often considered to be symbol of long-term vision and leadership — holding a quill pen. The unique merger of traditional Coast Salish eagle with the quill pen illustrates that the pathway to positive, sustainable change lies in our ability to acquire knowledge -- and share it with others." – *Louie Gong, Nooksack*

QUICK REFERENCE GUIDE

FOREWORD
UNDERSTANDING "INDIAN COUNTRY"

By RICHARD WALKER
Journalist

Within the boundaries of the United States of America are many nations.

The Constitution of the United States recognizes the inherent sovereignty of these indigenous nations, or as they are often called, Tribes; and it recognizes the power and authority of treaties the U.S. signed with them, making no distinction between a treaty signed with a Tribe and a treaty signed with Great Britain or Russia.

Article I, Section 8 of the Constitution states that Congress has the authority to "regulate commerce with foreign nations, and among several states, *and with the Indian Tribes." (my emphasis).*

Article VI of the Constitution states, "The constitution, and the laws of the United States which shall be made in Pursuance thereof; and all treaties made, or which shall be made under the authority of the United States, *shall be the supreme law of the land; and the judges in every State shall be bound thereby." (again, my emphasis).*

Some background: Governments that sent emissaries to this continent to claim land here knew they had to establish treaties with indigenous leaders in order to extinguish aboriginal title and make land available for settlement.

Some treaties were negotiated, some were forced. Nevertheless, leaders of those indigenous nations signed treaties which made land available for settlement, in exchange for certain payment and other considerations.

Out of the land to which they ceded ownership they retained land for themselves, much in the same way that sellers of property today might set aside land for themselves upon selling a vast tract. Indigenous treaty signers also retained certain rights in their historical territories, much as a seller of property today might retain certain rights, such as mineral rights or rights of way.

Those treaties laid the groundwork for the system of land ownership Americans enjoy today. However, indigenous treaty signers never ceded their nationhood. (If you buy land from the federal, state or local government, do those governments cease to exist as governmental entities?). Indigenous treaty signers did not cede their right to self-govern nor their access to certain resources within their traditional territories, including off-reservation. That's why Tribal governments within Washington co-manage the state's salmon fishery with the state government. It's why local development plans must be reviewed by Tribal governments if such development might impact streams and salmon. It's why indigenous governments have some say over potential impacts to, and have access to, shellfish beds that are on public and private tidelands.

In short, indigenous nations remained sovereign, or self-governing, nations. The U.S. Constitution and court decisions – too numerous to cite here – recognize and/or uphold indigenous nationhood. (My non-Indian grandfather was born in 1902 in Muskogee, Oklahoma, when it was Indian Territory. He was listed in subsequent censuses as "foreign born.")

Within the U.S., there are local governments, county governments, state governments, the federal government, and Tribal governments. Only two of those governments have the authority to grant citizenship: the U.S. government and Tribal governments. U.S. citizens are subject to the laws of the United States. Citizens of indigenous nations are dual citizens, subject to the laws of the United States and of their respective indigenous nations. When covering Indian Country, you are covering indigenous nations that have a special relationship with the United States and the authority of sovereign government.

Indian Country is complex. We hope this guide will help you understand Indian Country and help you in your reporting.

My colleagues and I welcome your feedback. Contact information is included in the Introduction.

– Richard Walker, Mexican/Yaqui, is an editor for Sound Publishing, Inc., and a correspondent for Indian Country Today Media Network.

INTRODUCTION

"If the many issues facing Indian country are not better known or understood, it is partly because the major media have failed to cover them properly," Thomas Vinciguerra wrote in Indian Country Today on April 8, 2013.

Vinciguerra was reporting on a panel discussion at the Graduate School of Journalism of Columbia University in New York City, titled "Who's Got Reservations? Journalism in Indian Country." The discussion offered a frank look at assumptions, misperceptions and double standards in the reporting of news involving America's indigenous peoples.

In Vinciguerra's story, William Grueskin, the journalism school's dean of academic affairs, said, "The way most media covers the Native American population is some kind of precipitating event... Either it's a crime or a study of alcoholism or the opening of a casino." Anishinaabe journalist Wab Kinew added, "Journalists are predisposed to choose stories that are familiar... It's much easier for a journalist to tell a story in the manner to which he is accustomed, rather than in a new and novel fashion." There was consensus that journalists have little understanding of the diversity and richness of Native America, Vinciguerra reported, and that lack of understanding affects reporting on Native America. This guide is designed to change that by helping editors, writers and journalists understand proper word usage, protocols, terminology, and important laws related to Indian Country.

The Indian Country Stylebook for Editors, Writers and Journalists is patterned after the Associated Press Stylebook for familiarity and ease of use. The guide contains more than 100 entries, with correct spellings, word usages, and legal references; a briefing on American

Indian Law; a briefing on news gathering in Indian Country; a directory of indigenous nations in Washington State; and a directory of Indian Country media in Washington State.

We hope this guide contributes to your appreciation and understanding of "the richness of Native culture and lives," and helps you as you strive for equity and accuracy in your reporting. Future editions are planned; we welcome your input and recommendations.

Richard Walker, richardmollywalker@gmail.com

Jackie Jacobs, jj@jtalentgroup.com

Gabriel Galanda, gabe@galandabroadman.com

Louie Gong, louielgong@gmail.com

STYLEBOOK

A

aboriginal, indigenous Same meaning. *Aboriginal* is used primarily in Canada. *Canada's aboriginal peoples. Indigenous* is preferred in the United States. *America's indigenous peoples. Indigenous peoples of the United States.*

Affiliated Tribes of Northwest Indians An organization of indigenous governments of the Northwest. Headquarters is in Portland. On second reference, *ATNI* may be used.

Alaska Native Claims Settlement Act Under the Alaska Native Claims Settlement Act, Alaska Natives reserved title to 44 million acres of land in Alaska and received $962 million in cash for the loss of other lands to the State. The Act established a system of village and regional Native corporations to manage the lands and cash payments, and made extensive provisions regarding the operations of the corporations.

American Indian, Alaska Native, Native Hawaiian Use *American Indian* or *Native American* to describe the indigenous peoples of the lower 48 states, *Alaska Native* to describe the indigenous peoples of Alaska, *Native Hawaiian* to describe the indigenous peoples of Hawaii. See *Native American, American Indian.*

assimilation   Cultural assimilation is the process by which a person or a people's language and/or culture come to resemble those of another group. In the case of America's indigenous peoples, there were many efforts to force assimilation through the years, including forced changes in lifestyle, the banning of cultural and religious ways, the forced enrollment of indigenous children in boarding schools.

B

Boldt decision   Formally known as *United States v. Washington,* a 1974 decision by U.S. District Court Judge George Hugo Boldt upholding Native treaty fishing rights. Boldt interpreted treaty language "in common with," regarding indigenous fishing rights, as meaning "sharing equally the opportunity to take fish." The decision upheld the right of Native fishers to 50 percent of the harvestable number of fish, and established treaty signatories as co-managers, with the state, of salmon and other fish species.

bones, remains   Use *remains* when referring to the remains of a human being.

C

canoe   Do not use *boat.* A Northwest canoe can be made of cedar, cedar strips, or fiberglass. Traditional dugout canoes were carved from a single cedar log. The other construction methods were adopted as larger cedar logs became scarce because of logging. Types of canoes include nearshore canoes; ocean-going, traveling or whaling canoes; racing and war canoes; and river or shovel-nose canoes. A nearshore canoe is ideal for use when harvesting shellfish. Ocean-going canoes have a raised prow and can be up to 50 feet long and carry entire families long distances. Racing canoes are different lengths and can hold a crew of one, two, six, or 11 pullers. A river or shovel-nose canoe has a rounded prow and stern and a flatter bottom to handle swift river currents.

canoe club, canoe family, canoe society   An organization which promotes the activities and values associated with traditional canoe culture. Values include commitment, generosity, honor, humility, respect, and personal responsibility. Activities include canoe races and the annual Canoe Journey.

Canoe Journey   An annual gathering of Northwest canoe cultures. *The Canoe Journey, 2013 Canoe Journey/Paddle to Quinault.* Acceptable in subsequent reference: *Paddle to Quinault.* The colloquial *Tribal Journeys* is acceptable in quotes.

Carcieri v. Salazar   A 2009 U.S. Supreme Court decision regarding the federal government taking land into trust from federally recognized Native Nations. The court ruled that the term "now under federal jurisdiction" referred to indigenous nations that were federally recognized when the Indian Reorganization Act of 1934 became law, and that the federal government could not therefore take land into trust from Tribes recognized after 1934. If the land is not taken into trust, local jurisdictions have land-use and taxation authority on said land, not the Native Nation that owns it.

Carcieri fix   Congressional legislation to authorize the U.S. Secretary of the Interior to take land into trust from specific Native Nations. Also, congressional legislation, pending in 2016, to amend the language of the Indian Reorganization Act of 1934.

chant   Do not use. Songs are songs, not chants. See *dance, drum, perform, sing.*

Chehalis Confederated Tribes *He is a citizen of the Chehalis Tribes. Jane Doe, Chehalis, spoke at the meeting. A group of Chehalis citizens.* The head of government is the chairman or chairwoman; the legislative body is the Chehalis Business Council. Government offices are located in Oakville. Dateline: *Oakville.*

Chief A formal, usually hereditary, title. Capitalize before subject's name. *Lummi Chief Tsilixw James. Tsilixw James, a hereditary chief of the Lummi Nation.*

Chinook *The Chinook Nation, the Chinook people, Chinook jargon.* But *chinook salmon.*

Chinook jargon A simplified trade language developed in the 1850s to facilitate communication between non-Native and Native peoples. Not to be confused with the Chinook language.

Coast Salish, Interior Salish Many of the indigenous nations of what is now Washington state are related linguistically and culturally, and are considered Coast Salish or Interior Salish. Most of the nations on the Salish Sea are Coast Salish. A good online resource showing locations and names of historic Coast Salish village sites is located at www.coastsalishmap.org

Colville Confederated Tribes *He is a citizen of the Colville Tribes. Jane Doe, Colville, spoke at the event. A group of Colville citizens.* The head of government is the chairman or chairwoman; the legislative body is the Colville Business Council. Government offices are located in Nespelem. Dateline: *Nespelem.*

Cowlitz Indian Tribe   *He is citizen of the Cowlitz Tribe. Jane Doe, Cowlitz, spoke at the meeting. A group of Cowlitz citizens.* The head of government is the chairman or chairwoman; the legislative body is the Cowlitz Tribal Council. Government offices are located in Longview. Dateline: *Longview.*

costume   Do not use. Articles of clothing worn in ceremonies and dances are called *regalia.* See *regalia* entry.

Creator   Capitalize when referring to God.

cultural appropriation   Use of the cultural or intellectual property belonging to another culture, usually by people who have no understanding of their cultural significance.

cultural property, intellectual property   Dances, regalia, songs, stories are often inherited and belong to the dancer, wearer, singer, storyteller.

D

dance, drum, perform, sing   Traditional dancing, drumming, and singing have a spiritual element and are often a form of prayer. A drummer *drums, offers* or *sings* a song; do not use *bangs a drum, plays a song,* or *chants.* A dancer *dances.* Do not use *perform.* A powwow dancer *competes* in a specific type of dance. *The drummer offered an honor song. She sang a canoe paddle song. Dressed in beaded regalia fringed with brightly colored yarn and ribbon, the men competed in the fast-paced grass dance at the powwow.*

datelines   See entry for each indigenous nation.

discover, discovered　Do not use when writing about the exploration era. *Explore, explored, exploration* are preferred terms.

E

enroll, enrollment　To *enroll* is to officially register as a member, or citizen, of an indigenous nation. Enrollment criteria are set forth in constitutions, articles of incorporation or ordinances of each indigenous nation, and the criterion varies. Common requirements for citizenship are lineal descendancy from someone named on the indigenous nation's base roll (the original list of citizens as designated in an indigenous nation's constitution or other document specifying enrollment criteria), and degree of ancestry (also known as blood quantum).

F

federal recognition　A formal recognition by the United States of America of an indigenous government, establishing a government to government relationship. Similar to U.S. recognition of a foreign government. Not all Tribes are federally recognized, and not all federally recognized Tribes are Treaty Tribes. For more information, go to the Governor's Office on Indian Affairs' website, www.GOIA.wa.gov.

First Nations　Use when referring to the indigenous nations and peoples of Canada. *Saanich First Nation. First Nations people.*

fishers　Use when referring to a group comprised of fishermen and fisherwomen.

Fish Wars A series of civil disobedience protests in the 1960s and 1970s, in which Native Americans pressured the U.S. government to recognize fishing rights granted by treaties. Native Americans refused to obtain fishing licenses from the state, arguing that their right to fish were derived from treaties with the U.S. government. The protests led to the lawsuit, *U.S. vs. Washington.* See *Boldt decision.*

funerary objects Objects placed with individual human remains either at the time of death or burial.

G

gambling Do not use when referring to traditional indigenous games, such as stick games. See *gaming.*

gaming Use when referring to traditional games, such as stick games and games offered by Native American gaming facilities or casinos. America's indigenous peoples have historically enjoyed games for amusement, competition and tests of skill; and for social purposes at gatherings, ceremonies and celebrations. Some indigenous games, such as sla-hal and lacrosse, were gifts from the Creator. The emphasis in *gaming* is social. The emphasis in *gambling* is money.

government-to-government relationship See *federal recognition.*

H

Hoh Tribe *He is a citizen of the Hoh Tribe. Jane Doe, Hoh Tribe, spoke at the meeting. A group of Hoh Tribe citizens.* The head of government is the chairman or chairwoman; the legislative body is the Hoh Tribe Business Committee. Government offices are located on the Hoh Reservation; the mailing address is Forks. Dateline: *Hoh.*

honor poles, story poles, totem poles, etc. Various types of poles are carved in the Pacific Northwest and displayed to serve various purposes.

An *honor pole* honors an individual or family; a *mortuary pole* memorializes someone who has passed away; a *story pole* tells the story of an event or a place.

A *shaming pole* was intended to shame an individual or family that owed an unpaid debt. The pole might face the individual or family's house. Once the debt was paid, the pole was turned around to face the water, with the addition of totems representing wealth.

A *totem pole* is carved with a series of totemic symbols representing family lineage and events.

A *welcome pole* is used to welcome guests, and usually features a figure with hands raised in welcome.

house posts The interior posts of a longhouse, usually carved to tell the story of the family that owned the house or to tell stories important to the local culture. See *honor poles, story poles, totem poles.*

I

Indian, Indians Technically, it is inaccurate to refer to the indigenous people of this continent as "Indians." Indians are from India. Theories of how the "Indian" reference began typically refer to the 1492 voyage of Columbus, when he thought he had landed in India. Others conjecture the name is a derivation of the Spanish term, *indios*. Regardless, the name has stuck, sufficiently so that many indigenous people here refer to themselves as such and have used the term when establishing organizations such as the National Congress of American Indians or the Affiliated Tribes of Northwest Indians.

Indian Arts and Crafts Act of 1990 A truth-in-advertising law (P.L. 101-644) that prohibits misrepresentation in marketing of Native American art and craft works within the United States. It is illegal to offer or display for sale, or sell any art or craft product in a manner that falsely suggests it is Native American-produced, a Native American product, or the product of a particular Native American individual, indigenous nation, or Native American arts and crafts organization, resident within the United States. Under the Act, a Native American or American Indian is defined as a member of any federally or officially state-recognized indigenous nation, or an individual certified as a Native artisan by an indigenous nation. See *Native art, Native-style art.*

Indian Country As defined in 18 USC 1151, Indian Country is "(a) all land within the limits of any Indian reservation under the jurisdiction of the United States Government, notwithstanding the issuance of any patent, and, including rights-of-way running through the reservation, (b) all dependent Indian communities within the borders of the United States whether within the original or subsequently acquired territory thereof, and whether within or without the limits of a state, and (c) all Indian allotments, the Indian titles to which have not been extinguished, including rights-of-way running through the same."

Indian Shaker Church A Christian denomination founded in 1881 by John Slocum, Squaxin, who received a vision during a near-death experience. The Indian Shaker Church is a unique blend of American indigenous, Catholic, and Protestant beliefs and practices. The Indian Shakers are unrelated to the Shakers of New England

(United Society of Believers).

inherent rights   Rights bestowed upon the First Peoples by the Creator who placed them here and provided them with instruction on how to live. "The Creator's instruction formed the basis of the traditional knowledge, culture, traditions and oral traditions that have directed First Nations ever since," Bob Joseph, Gwawaenuk Nation, wrote on the Indigenous Corporate Training Inc. website. "Therefore, First Nation inherent rights are not granted by the [government]." Inherent rights "commonly include right to self-government, rights to the land, and right to practice their own culture and customs."

In Canada, inherent rights are protected under Section 25 of the Canadian Charter of Human Rights, guaranteeing "any rights or freedoms that have been recognized by the Royal Proclamation of October 7, 1763; and any rights or freedoms that now exist by way of land claims agreements or may be so acquired."

In the United States, inherent rights are recognized by the Declaration of Independence, ("the right to life, liberty and the pursuit of happiness") and are protected under the Fifth and 14th Amendments to the U.S. Constitution.

inherited rights   See *cultural property, intellectual property*.

J

Jamestown S'Klallam Tribe   *He is a citizen of the Jamestown S'Klallam Tribe. Jane Doe, Jamestown S'Klallam, spoke at the meeting. A group of Jamestown S'Klallam citizens.* The head of government is the chairman or chairwoman; the legislative body is the Jamestown S'Klallam Tribal Council. Government offices are located in Blyn; the mailing address is Sequim. Dateline: *Blyn*.

K

Kalispel Tribe   *He is a citizen of the Kalispel Tribe. Jane Doe, Kalispel, spoke at the meeting. A group of Kalispel Tribe citizens.* The head of government is the chairman or chairwoman; the legislative body is the Kalispel Business Council. Government offices are located in Usk. Dateline: *Kalispel.*

L

landless tribes   Do not use except in direct quotes or in context of court decisions affecting indigenous nations with reservations. Many indigenous nations that do not have reservations, such as the Samish Indian Nation, have acquired land and are thus not landless. See *Boldt decision.*

legend   Do not use when referring to cultural stories. Use *stories.* See *myths.*

longhouse   Historically, a house occupied by several families, usually closely related. As in historical times, modern longhouses are venues for events, gatherings and ceremonies, such as potlatches. See *smokehouse.*

Lower Elwha Klallam Tribe   *He is a citizen of the Lower Elwha Klallam Tribe. Jane Doe, Elwha Klallam, spoke at the meeting. A group of Elwha Klallam citizens.* The head of government is the chairman or chairwoman; the legislative body is the Lower Elwha Tribal Council. Government offices are located on the Lower Elwha Klallam Reservation; the mailing address is Port Angeles. Dateline: *Lower Elwha Klallam.*

Lummi Nation   *He is a citizen of the Lummi Nation. Jane Doe, Lummi, spoke at the meeting. A group of Lummi citizens.* The head of government is the chairman or chairwoman; the legislative body is the Lummi Indian Business Council. Government offices are located on the Lummi Nation Reservation; the mailing address is Bellingham. Dateline: *Lummi Nation.*

Lushootseed   A Coast Salish language, divided into *Northern Lushootseed* and *Southern Lushootseed,* or *Whulshootseed,* based on vocabulary and stress patterns.

M

Makah Nation   *He is a citizen of the Makah Nation. Jane Doe, Makah, spoke at the meeting. A group of Makah citizens.* The head of government is the chairman or chairwoman; the legislative body is the Makah Tribal Council. Government offices are located in Neah Bay. Dateline: *Neah Bay.*

master carver, master weaver   An individual who is widely considered to have mastered the art of carving or weaving, is widely considered an expert in their medium, and is often consulted as an authority or instructor. *Lummi master carver Jewell Praying Wolf James. Samish master carver Tsul-ton, also known as William Bailey.*

Muckleshoot Indian Tribe   *He is a citizen of the Muckleshoot Tribe. Jane Doe, Muckleshoot, spoke at the meeting. A group of*

Muckleshoot citizens. The head of government is the chairman or chairwoman; the legislative body is the Muckleshoot Tribal Council. Government offices are located on the Muckleshoot Reservation; the mailing address is Auburn. Dateline: *Muckleshoot.*

myth   Do not use when describing cultural stories. *Myth* is widely understood to mean an idea or story that is believed by many people but is not true. Indigenous stories are based on fact, using terms and descriptions familiar to the people when the story developed. *The S'Klallam creation story. She shared the story of S'Klallam's creation.* See *Thunderbird.*

N

NAGPRA   Native American Graves Protection and Repatriation Act (25 USC 3001). On second reference, *NAGPRA.*

Native   Capitalize when referring to an indigenous person or people, lowercase when referring to animals and plants native to an area. *An audience comprised of Native and non-Native peoples.*

Native American, American Indian   Use the subject's preference. Whenever possible, refer to the subject by his or her Nation. *John Doe, Lummi.*

Native American Church   A Native American religion sometimes characterized by mixed indigenous and Christian beliefs and sometimes by the sacramental use of peyote. Native American use of peyote for religious purposes is protected by the American Indian Religious Freedom Act Amendments of 1994.

Native art, Native-style art　　Use *Native art* when referring to art made by a Native American artist. Use *Native-style art* when referring to such art made by a non-Native artist.

Native Hawaiian　　Any individual who is a descendant of the aboriginal people who, prior to 1778, occupied and exercised sovereignty in the area that now constitutes the State of Hawaii. [25 USC 3001 (10)]

Native peoples　　A collective term for more than one group of indigenous peoples.

Nisqually Indian Tribe　　*He is a citizen of the Nisqually Tribe. Jane Doe, Nisqually, spoke at the meeting. A group of Nisqually Tribe citizens.* The head of government is the chairman or chairwoman; the legislative body is the Nisqually Tribal Council. Government offices are located on the Nisqually Reservation; the mailing address is Olympia. Dateline: *Nisqually.*

NDN　　Shorthand spelling for Indian, a common term that Native Americans use to refer to themselves. Use NDN when quoting written works.

Nooksack Indian Tribe　　*He is a citizen of the Nooksack Tribe. Jane Doe, Nooksack, spoke at the meeting. A group of Nooksack citizens.* The head of government is the chairman or chairwoman; the legislative body is the Nooksack Tribal Council. Government offices are located on the Nooksack Reservation; the mailing address is Deming. Dateline: *Nooksack.*

Northwest Coast art, Coast Salish art　　Northwest Coast art is a style of art created by First Nation and Native American artists of the Northwest Coast; it is distinguished by the use of ovoids (rounded rectangle shape), and U-shapes. Coast Salish art is a style of art created by artists from Coast Salish nations; it is distinguished by the use of crescents, ovals and trigons.

Northwest Indian College   An accredited college offering two- and four-year degrees. The main campus is on the Lummi Nation reservation. Satellite campuses are located at Muckleshoot, Nez Perce, Nisqually, Port Gamble S'Klallam, Swinomish, Tulalip.

Northwest Indian Fisheries Commission   An organization of 20 treaty Tribes in Western Washington. Its headquarters are in Olympia, with offices in Burlington and Forks. Use *NWIFC* in second reference. The NWIFC was created following the decision in U.S. v. Washington, which re-affirmed treaty-reserved fishing rights and established treaty signatories as fisheries co-managers with the State of Washington. The NWIFC assists its members in their role as fisheries co-managers.

NorthWest Indian News   A news program produced by the Tulalip Tribes and aired on at least 17 stations in the Pacific Northwest, It can also be viewed online at nwin.tv. The W is capitalized. Use *NWIN* in second reference.

Northwest Intertribal Court System   A consortium which provides administrative, appellate, code development, information technology, judicial and prosecution services for courts of indigenous nations in Washington state. Its headquarters is in Lynnwood.

O

offensive terms   Do not use *redskin* or *squaw* except in direct quotes, and then only when their use is an integral, essential part of the story; both of these terms have historically demeaning applications and origins. *Brave* and *buckskin* are considered offensive when used to refer to individuals of indigenous ancestry. However, *Braves* can be acceptable when referring to a sports team of that name. *The LaConner Braves. Buckskin* is acceptable when referring to a division in canoe racing.

An Abenaki anthropologist on the word 'squaw'

In her 1999 essay, "Reclaiming 'squaw' in the name of the ancestors," Dr. Margaret Bruchac, Abenaki, assistant professor of anthropology at the University of Pennsylvania, explains how "squaw" came to be widely viewed as a hurtful term.

Bruchac writes that the word "squaw" is a phonetic rendering of an Algonkian word, or morpheme, "variously spelled 'squa,' 'skwa,' 'esqua,' 'kwe,' 'squeh,' 'kw' etc. ... used to indicate 'female.'"

She writes, "During the late 19th century, Algonkian words that had come into common usage among Americans were carried west, by French fur traders and other whites ... During westward expansion, 'chief,' 'brave,' 'papoose,' and 'squaw' took on negative connotations as they were increasingly used as generic descriptions and epithets." The misappropriation and misuse of the word "squaw" was further spread by early 20th century films and books that depicted and perpetuated stereotypes.

Dr. Bruchac writes that the word "squaw" is an Algonkian word and is "neither historically nor linguistically appropriate as a universal term to apply to Native women." She adds, "We, as indigenous people, must not let other cultures define, and abuse, our history, languages and symbols."

Oliphant vs. Suquamish Indian Tribe
A 1978 court case filed by a non-Native resident of the Port Madison Indian Reservation who had been arrested and charged by Tribal police with assaulting a Tribal police officer and resisting arrest. The plaintiff challenged the existence of Tribal authority over non-Indians. The challenge was rejected by lower courts, which ruled that law enforcement was an attribute of sovereignty that was neither surrendered by treaty nor removed by the U.S. Congress under its plenary power. The U.S.

Supreme Court ruled 7-2 for the plaintiff, determining that Tribal courts do not have inherent criminal jurisdiction over non-Indians and may not assume such jurisdiction unless specifically authorized to do so by Congress. See *Violence Against Women Act* for an example of Congressional authorization.

P

political titles   The titles of heads of indigenous governments vary; *i.e., Quinault Nation President Fawn Sharp, Swinomish Tribe Chairman Brian Cladoosby.* See *Directory of Indigenous Nations in Washington State.*

Port Gamble S'Klallam Tribe   *He is a citizen of the Port Gamble S'Klallam Tribe. Jane Doe, Port Gamble S'Klallam, spoke at the meeting. A group of Port Gamble S'Klallam citizens.* The head of government is the chairman or chairwoman, the legislative body is the Port Gamble S'Klallam Tribal Council. Government offices are located in Little Boston; the mailing address is Kingston. Dateline: *Little Boston.*

potlatch   A hosted gathering to celebrate a significant life event or honor the memory of someone who passed away. Historically, gifting during potlatches was a system of wealth distribution. In addition, the more wealth that the host gave away in gifting, the more prestige was bestowed on him or her.

power   A gift, usually spiritual, which endows the individual with unique abilities. Obtained usually after a period of spiritual preparation, which may include fasting and prayer. See *shaman.*

powwow   Also pow-wow, pow wow. A powwow is a social gathering and celebration of cultures. Many dances and songs are sacred; ask permission before photographing or recording.

Public Law 83-280   Also known as PL 83-280, enacted in 1953, transferred certain federal, civil and criminal jurisdiction over Indian Country to six states on a mandatory basis and allowed other states to assume complete or partial jurisdiction in the same manner, all without the consent of the Tribes involved. Washington, which was not one of the mandatory states, assumed some jurisdiction in 1957, with Tribal consent; and again in 1963, without tribal consent. In 1968, the Indian Civil Rights Act amended PL 280 to require Tribal consent before any more states could assume federal jurisdiction. It also allowed states to retrocede, or return jurisdiction. *See retrocession.*

pullers   Use *pullers* when referring to the crew of a racing or traveling canoe. *Pullers* is used because of the pulling motion on the canoe paddle. *Paddlers* is acceptable. Do not use *rowers*.

Puyallup Tribe   *He is a citizen of the Puyallup Tribe. Jane Doe, Puyallup, spoke at the meeting. A group of Puyallup citizens.* The head of government is the chairman or chairwoman; the legislative body is the Puyallup Tribal Council. Government offices are located on the Puyallup Reservation; the mailing address is Tacoma. Dateline: *Puyallup.*

Q

Quileute Tribe   *He is a citizen of the Quileute Tribe. Jane Doe, Quileute, spoke at the meeting. A group of Quileute citizens.* The head of government is the chairman or chairwoman; the legislative body is the Quileute Tribal Council. Government offices are located in La Push. Dateline: *La Push.*

Quinault Nation *He is a citizen of the Quinault Nation. Jane Doe, Quinault, spoke at the meeting. A group of Quinault citizens.* The head of government is the president; the legislative body is the Quinault Tribal Council. Government offices are located in Taholah. Dateline: *Taholah.*

R

Rafeedie decision A 1994 ruling by U.S. District Court Judge Edward Rafeedie. He ruled that all public and private tidelands are subject to treaty harvest, except for shellfish contained in artificially created beds. His decision requires Tribes planning to harvest shellfish from private beaches to follow many time, place, and manner restrictions on harvest.

regalia Traditional clothing worn in ceremonies and dances. Regalia or regalia items may be gifted or inherited and often have spiritual significance. *The dancer wore a bustle made of eagle feathers. The speaker wore a hat and vest made of woven cedar fiber.* Ask the wearer for names and materials of particular articles. Ask permission to photograph.

repatriation The return of human remains or cultural objects to their place of origin.

reservation Land reserved by and for an indigenous nation or nations, usually by treaty and usually held in trust by the United States. Use *rez* in direct quotes. Note: Many reservations were established for several indigenous groups. For example, the Tulalip reservation was set aside for the Snohomish, Snoqualmie and Stllaguamish, and some people living at Tulalip identify by their ancestral group.

retrocession   The process established by the State of Washington in which Tribal governments can ask for the return of jurisdiction over certain civil and criminal matters. The process was established by HB 2233, signed into law by Gov. Christine Gregoire in 2012. *See Public Law 83-280.*

S

sacred   An object or site having special spiritual significance.

Samish Indian Nation   *He is a citizen of the Samish Nation. Jane Doe, Samish, spoke at the meeting. A group of Samish citizens.* The head of government is the chairman or chairwoman; the legislative body is the Samish Tribal Council. Government offices are in Anacortes. Dateline: *Anacortes.*

Sauk-Suiattle Tribe   *He is a citizen of the Sauk-Suiattle Tribe. Jane Doe, Sauk-Suiattle, spoke at the meeting. A group of Sauk-Suiattle citizens.* The head of government is the chairman or chairwoman; the legislative body is the Sauk-Suiattle Tribal Council. Government offices are on the Sauk-Suiattle Reservation; the mailing address is Darrington. Dateline: *Sauk-Suiattle.*

self-government   See *sovereign, sovereignty.*

Seowyn   A spiritual faith practiced by Coast Salish people, which includes longhouse ceremonies during winter. Individuals initiated into Seowyn are called *initiates.*

shaman   *Healer* is preferred. An individual with the power to cure the sick and conduct other interventions.

Shoalwater Bay Tribe   *He is a citizen of the Shoalwater Bay Tribe. Jane Doe, Shoalwater Bay Tribe, spoke at the meeting. A group of Shoalwater Bay Tribe citizens.* The head of government is the chairman or chairwoman; the legislative body is the Shoalwater Bay Tribal Council. Government offices are on the Shoalwater Bay Reservation; the mailing address is Tokeland. Dateline: *Shoalwater Bay.*

S'Klallam   Indigenous people of the northern coast of the Olympic Peninsula. *Jamestown S'Klallam* and *Port Gamble S'Klallam,* but *Lower Elwha Klallam* or *Elwha Klallam.*

Skokomish Tribe   *He is a citizen of the Skokomish Tribe. Jane Doe, Skokomish, spoke at the meeting. A group of Skokomish citizens.* The head of government is the chairman or chairwoman; the legislative body is the Skokomish Tribal Council. Government offices are on the Skokomish Reservation; the mailing address is Shelton. Dateline: *Skokomish.*

sla-hal   A game, also known as bone game or stick game, played with game pieces and tally sticks historically made from animal bone. The game is played with two opposing teams. There are two sets of game pieces, or bones, two sets of sticks and a kick or king stick — an extra stick won by the team who gets to start the game. When a game is in play, one of the two teams will have two sets of bones. Two individuals will hide the bones and swap them around from hand to hand; the objective is to make sure the other team guesses wrong on which hand has the bones. When the other team guesses incorrectly, the team with the bones gain a point. The game is accompanied by drumming and singing used to boost the morale of the team, and sometimes to taunt the other team. The side that has the bones sings, while the other tries to guess.

smokehouse A modern longhouse in which open fires may be lighted. Like a longhouse, a smokehouse is a venue for events, gatherings and ceremonies, such as potlatches. Not to be confused with a smokehouse used for smoking salmon.

Snoqualmie Tribe *He is a citizen of the Snoqualmie Tribe. Jane Doe, Snoqualmie Tribe, spoke at the meeting. A group of Snoqualmie Tribe citizens.* The head of government is the chairman or chairwoman, the legislative body is the Snoqualmie Tribal Council. Government offices are on the Snoqualmie Reservation. Dateline: *Snoqualmie.*

Sohappy v. Smith A 1969 U.S. District Court case, combined with United States v. Oregon, which upheld the right of signatories to 1855 treaties to fish in the Columbia River. The Confederated Tribes of the Umatilla Indian Reservation, the Confederated Tribes of the Warm Springs Reservation of Oregon, the Confederated Tribes and Bands of the Yakama Nation, and the Nez Perce Tribe founded the Columbia River Inter-Tribal Fish Commission in 1977 to work with the state and federal governments in fisheries management, habitat restoration, and treaty rights protection on the Columbia River.

sovereign, sovereignty Having ultimate authority over land and territory.

Spokane Tribe *He is a citizen of the Spokane Tribe. Jane Doe, Spokane Tribe, spoke at the meeting. A group of Spokane Tribe citizens.* The head of government is the chairman or chairwoman; the legislative body is the Spokane Tribal Business Council. Government offices are in Wellpinit. Dateline: *Wellpinit.*

Squaxin Island Tribe *He is a citizen of the Squaxin Island Tribe. Jane Doe, Squaxin, spoke at the meeting. A group of Squaxin Island Tribe* *citizens.* The head of government is the chairman or chairwoman; the legislative body is the Squaxin Island Tribal Council. Government offices are on the Squaxin Reservation; the mailing address is Shelton. Dateline: *Squaxin.*

state recognition The State of Washington does not have a government-to-government relationship with indigenous nations not recognized by the United States. See *federal recognition*

Stillaguamish Tribe *He is a citizen of the Stillaguamish Tribe. Jane Doe, Stillaguamish, spoke at the meeting. A group of Stillaguamish citizens.* The head of government is the chairman or chairwoman; the legislative body is the Stillaguamish Board of Directors. Government offices are on the Stillaguamish Reservation; the mailing address is Arlington. Dateline: *Stillaguamish.*

Suquamish Tribe *He is a citizen of the Suquamish Tribe. Jane Doe, Suquamish, spoke at the meeting. A group of Suquamish citizens.* The head of government is the chairman or chairwoman; the legislative body is the Suquamish Tribal Council. Government offices are in Suquamish. Dateline: *Suquamish.*

Swinomish Indian Tribal Community *Swinomish Tribe* is OK in all references. *He is a citizen of the Swinomish Tribe. Jane Doe, Swinomish, spoke at the meeting. A group of Swinomish citizens.* The head of government is the chairman or chairwoman; the legislative body is the Swinomish Tribal Senate. Government offices are in Swinomish Village; the mailing address is La Conner. Dateline: *Swinomish.*

T

Thunderbird   A supernatural bird of power and strength. Thunderbird is found in stories about major natural events. In the 1990s, a University of Washington geologist determined that a traditional story about Thunderbird struggling with and seizing a whale, which was killing other whales and depriving the people of meat and oil – "The waters receded and rose again. Many canoes came down in trees and were destroyed and numerous lives were lost" – may describe an actual catastrophic event, a tsunami in 1700.

tipi   A type of home, made of poles and hide, and historically used in what is now Washington state by Plains peoples, such as the Spokane and Yakama.

Tribal citizen   See next entry.

Tribal member   *Citizen* is preferred. Citizens, or members, of Tribes are actually dual citizens who are subject to the authority of the United States and of their respective indigenous nation. In the United States, only the U.S. and indigenous nations have the authority to confer citizenship. *He is a citizen of the Quinault Nation. She is a citizen of the Shoalwater Bay Tribe.*

Tribal Sovereignty Curriculum   Curriculum adopted by the Washington State Office of Superintendent of Public Instruction in response to a 2005 state law, HB 1495, that encourages Washington school districts to teach history, culture and governance of indigenous nations in Washington. SB 5433, signed into law on May 8, 2015, requires the teaching about history, culture and governance of indigenous nations in Washington. As of this publication, the curriculum *"Since Time Immemorial: Tribal Sovereignty in*

Washington State," is the only curriculum available that is aligned with Washington State education standards. See www.Indian-Ed.org.

Tribe   A term first used during the colonial era to characterize indigenous nations. Capitalize *Tribe* to distinguish between a Native Nation and a group of people linked by culture, ethnicity, kinship, politics or religion. Use when part of the indigenous nation's formal name. Otherwise, use the nation's name for itself. *Hoh Tribe, Quinault Nation, Samish Indian Nation*

Tsonokwa   also *Tsonoqua* or, in Kwakwaka'wakw, *Dzunukwa*. The name of the "wild woman of the forest." In some Northwest Native cultures, she is venerated as a bringer of wealth and fortune to those who encounter and befriend her, but she is also greatly feared by children because she carries a huge basket on her back in which she puts disobedient children and takes them to her home. The 'Namgis people say she will lure a child by imitating the child's grandmother's voice. Her call, "Hu!," sounds like the wind blowing through the trees. However, she walks with a shuffle and has poor eyesight, and can be avoided or outwitted. A similar being in S'Klallam territory is known as Slapoo.

Tulalip Tribes   *He is a citizen of the Tulalip Tribes. Jane Doe, Tulalip, spoke at the meeting. A group of Tulalip citizens.* When referring to the nation, use *The Tulalip Tribes is,* not *The Tulalip Tribes are.* The head of government is the chairman or chairwoman; the legislative body is the Tulalip Board of Directors. Government offices are in Tulalip. Dateline: *Tulalip.*

U

Usual and Accustomed Area   A Tribe's historical region in which it harvested finfish, shellfish, and other natural resources. Treaty Tribes have the right to harvest finfish, shellfish, and other natural resources within their usual and accustomed area. Use *U&A* in subsequent reference. See *Rafeedie decision.*

Upper Skagit Tribe *He is a citizen of the Upper Skagit Tribe. Jane Doe, Upper Skagit, spoke at the meeting. A group of Upper Skagit citizens.* The head of government is the chairman or chairwoman; the legislative body is the Upper Skagit Tribal Council. Government offices are on the Upper Skagit Reservation; the mailing address is Sedro-Woolley. Dateline: *Upper Skagit.*

V

Violence Against Women Act The 2013 update of federal law, approved by the U.S. Congress, which gives Tribal governments authority to prosecute anyone – Native and non-Native – for violent crimes committed against women on Tribal lands. *VAWA* is OK in subsequent reference.

W

Washington Indian Gaming Association A trade association of indigenous nations that have gaming as part of their economic development portfolio. Its headquarters is in Olympia.

X

No entries

Y

Yakama Nation   *He is a citizen of the Yakama Nation. Jane Doe, Yakama, spoke at the meeting. A group of Yakama citizens.* The head of government is the chairman or chairwoman; the legislative body is the Yakama Nation Tribal Council. Government offices are in Toppenish. Dateline: *Toppenish.* Note different spelling of city and county of *Yakima.*

Yakama Nation Review   The newspaper of the Yakama Nation. Its offices are in Toppenish.

Z

No entries

DIRECTORY OF INDIGENOUS NATIONS IN WASHINGTON STATE

Chehalis Confederated Tribes

420 Howanut Road
Oakville, WA 98568
360-273-5911/360-753-3213

County: Grays Harbor, Thurston
Online: www.chehalistribe.org
Head of government: Chairman or chairwoman
Legislative body: Chehalis Business Council
Treaty: Proposed treaties rejected by the Chehalis people;
reservation established by the United States government in 1860.
Language: Chehalis

Colville Confederated Tribes

P.O. Box 150
Nespelem, WA 99155
509-634-2200

County: Okanogan, Ferry
Online: www.colvilletribes.com
Head of government: Chairman or chairwoman
Legislative body: Colville Business Council
Treaty: Reservation established by executive order of the president
of the United States on April 19, 1872.
Language: Okanagan

Cowlitz Indian Tribe
1055 9th Ave., Suite B
Longview, WA 98632
360-577-8140

County: Cowlitz/Clark
Online: www.cowlitz.org
Head of government: Chairman or chairwoman
Legislative body: Cowlitz Tribal Council
Treaty: Participated in negotiations of, but declined to sign,
Chehalis River Treaty of 1855; formally recognized by U.S. in 2000.
Language: Cowlitz

Hoh Tribe
2464 Lower Hoh Road
Forks, WA 98331
360-374-3271

County: Jefferson
Online: www.hohtribe-nsn.org
Head of government: Chairman or chairwoman
Legislative body: Hoh Tribe Business Committee
Treaty: Quinault River Treaty, 1856
Language: Quileute or Quillayute, the last living language of the
Chimakuan family of languages.

Jamestown S'Klallam Tribe
1033 Old Blyn Highway
Sequim, WA 98382
360-683-1109

County: Clallam
Online: www.jamestowntribe.org
Head of government: Chairman or chairwoman
Legislative body: Jamestown S'Klallam Tribal Council
Treaty: Treaty of Point No Point, 1855
Language: S'Klallam

Kalispel Tribe

P.O. Box 39
Usk, WA 99180
509-445-1147

County: Pend Oreille
Online: www.kalispeltribe.com
Head of government: Chairman or chairwoman
Legislative body: Kalispel Business Council
Treaty: Treaty proposed by Congress in 1872 rejected by Kalispel;
reservation established on allotted land in 1914.
Language: Kalispel

Lower Elwha Klallam Tribe

2851 Lower Elwha Road
Port Angeles, WA 98363
360-452-8471

County: Clallam
Online: www.elwha.org
Head of government: Chairman or chairwoman
Legislative body: Lower Elwha Tribal Council
Treaty: Treaty of Point No Point, 1855
Language: S'Klallam

Lummi Nation

2616 Kwina Road
Bellingham, WA 98226
360-384-1489

County: Whatcom
Online: www.lummi-nsn.org
Head of government: Chairman or chairwoman
Legislative body: Lummi Indian Business Council
Treaty: Treaty of Point Elliott, 1855
Language: Xwlemi Chosen

Makah Nation

P.O. Box 115
Neah Bay, WA 98357
360-645-2201

County: Clallam
Online: www.makah.com
Head of government: Chairman or chairwoman
Legislative body: Makah Tribal Council
Treaty: Treaty of Neah Bay, 1855
Language: Makah

Muckleshoot Indian Tribe

39015 172nd Ave. SE
Auburn, WA 98092
253-939-3311

County: King
Online: www.muckleshoot.nsn.us
Head of government: Chairman or chairwoman
Legislative body: Muckleshoot Tribal Council
Treaty: Treaty of Point Elliott 1855
Language: Whulshootseed

Nisqually Indian Tribe

4820 She-Nah-Num Drive SE
Olympia, WA 98513
360-456-5221

County: Thurston
Online: www.nisqually-nsn.gov
Head of government: Chairman or chairwoman
Legislative body: Nisqually Tribal Council
Treaty: Treaty of Medicine Creek, 1854
Language: Whulshootseed

Nooksack Indian Tribe
4979 Mount Baker Highway, Suite F
Deming, WA 98244
360-592-5164

County: Whatcom
Online: www.nooksacktribe.org
Head of government: Chairman or chairwoman
Legislative body: Nooksack Tribal Council
Treaty: Treaty of Point Elliott, 1855
Language: Lhéchalosem

Port Gamble S'Klallam Tribe
31912 Little Boston Road NE
Kingston, WA 98346
360-297-2646

County: Kitsap
Online: www.pgst.nsn.us
Head of government: Chairman or chairwoman
Legislative body: Port Gamble S'Klallam Tribal Council
Treaty: Treaty of Point No Point, 1855
Language: S'Klallam

Puyallup Tribe
3009 E. Portland Ave.
Tacoma, WA 98404
253-573-7800

County: Pierce
Online: www.puyallup-tribe.com
Head of government: Chairman or chairwoman
Legislative body: Puyallup Tribal Council
Treaty: Treaty of Medicine Creek, 1854
Language: Twulshootseed

Quileute Tribe

P.O. Box 279
La Push, WA 98350
360-374-6163

County: Clallam
Online: www.quileutenation.org
Head of government: Chairman or chairwoman
Legislative body: Quileute Tribal Council
Treaty: Quinault River Treaty, 1856
Language: Quileute or Quillayute, the last living language of the
Chimakuan family of languages.

Quinault Nation

P.O. Box 189
Taholah, WA 98587
360-276-8211

County: Grays Harbor, Jefferson
Online: www.quinaultindiannation.com
Head of government: President
Legislative body: Quinault Tribal Council
Treaty: Quinault River Treaty, 1856
Language: Quinault

Samish Indian Nation

2918 Commercial Ave.
P.O. Box 217
Anacortes, WA 98221
360-293-6404

County: Skagit
Online: www.samishtribe.nsn.us
Head of government: Chairman or chairwoman
Legislative body: Samish Tribal Council
Treaty: Treaty of Point Elliott, 1855
Language: Lkungen

Sauk-Suiattle Indian Tribe

5318 Chief Brown Lane
Darrington, WA 98241
360-436-0131

County: Skagit
Online: www.sauk-suiattle.com
Head of government: Chairman or chairwoman
Legislative body: Sauk-Suiattle Tribal Council
Treaty: Treaty of Point Elliott, 1855
Language: Lushootseed

Shoalwater Bay Tribe

P.O. Box 130
Tokeland, WA 98590
360-267-6766

County: Pacific
Online: www.shoalwaterbay-nsn.gov
Head of government: Chairman or chairwoman
Legislative body: Shoalwater Bay Tribal Council
Treaty: Reservation created by executive order of the president of
the United States on Sept. 22, 1866.
Language: Chinookan

Skokomish Tribe

N. 80 Tribal Center Road
Shelton, WA 98584
360-426-4232

County: Mason
Online: www.skokomish.org
Head of government: Chairman or chairwoman
Legislative body: Skokomish Tribal Council
Treaty: Treaty of Point No Point 1855
Language: Twana

Snoqualmie Tribe
P.O. Box 969
Snoqualmie, WA 98065
425-888-6551

County: King
Online: www.snoqualmienation.com
Head of government: Chairman or chairwoman
Legislative body: Snoqualmie Tribal Council
Treaty: Treaty of Point Elliott, 1855
Language: Whulshootseed

Spokane Tribe
P.O. Box 100
Wellpinit, WA 99040
509-458-6500

County: Stevens, Spokane
Online: www.spokanetribe.com
Head of government: Chairman or chairwoman
Legislative body: Spokane Tribal Business Council
Treaty: Peace Treaty of 1858
Language: Spokan, or Spokane

Squaxin Island Tribe
10 SE Squaxin Lane
Shelton, WA 98584
360-426-9781

County: Mason, Thurston
Online: www.squaxinisland.org
Head of government: Chairman or chairwoman
Legislative body: Squaxin Island Tribal Council
Treaty: Treaty of Medicine Creek, 1854
Language: Whulshootseed

Stillaguamish Tribe

P.O. Box 277
Arlington, WA 98223-0297
360-652-7362

County: Snohomish
Online: www.stillaguamish.com
Head of government: Chairman or chairwoman
Legislative body: Stillaguamish Board of Directors
Treaty: Treaty of Point Elliott, 1855
Language: Lushootseed

Suquamish Tribe

P.O. Box 498
Suquamish, WA 98392-0498
360-598-3311

County: Kitsap
Online: www.suquamish.nsn.us
Head of government: Chairman or chairwoman
Legislative body: Suquamish Tribal Council
Treaty: Treaty of Point Elliott, 1855
Language: Whulshootseed

Swinomish Indian Tribal Community

11404 Moorage Way
La Conner, WA 98257
360-466-3163

County: Skagit
Online: www.swinomish.nsn.us
Head of government: Chairman or chairwoman
Legislative body: Swinomish Tribal Senate
Treaty: Treaty of Point Elliott, 1855
Language: Swinomish, Lushootseed

Tulalip Tribes

6406 Marine Drive
Tulalip, WA 98271
360-716-4300

County: Snohomish
Online: www.tulaliptribes-nsn.gov
Head of government: Chairman or chairwoman
Legislative body: Tulalip Board of Directors
Treaty: Treaty of Point Elliott, 1855
Language: Lushootseed

Upper Skagit Tribe

25944 Community Plaza
Sedro-Woolley, WA 98284
360-854-7000

County: Skagit
Online: n/a
Head of government: Chairman or chairwoman
Legislative body: Upper Skagit Tribal Council
Treaty: Treaty of Point Elliott, 1855
Language: Lushootseed

Yakama Nation

P.O. Box 151
Toppenish, WA 98948
509-865-5121

County: Yakima, Klickitat
Online: www.yakamanation-nsn.gov
Head of government: Chairman or chairwoman
Legislative body: Yakama Nation Tribal Council
Treaty: Treaty with the Yakama, 1855
Language: Sahaptin; Ichishkíin Sínwit preferred

OTHER INDIGENOUS NATIONS

*Those that do not have a relationship with the
U.S. government (non-recognized)*

Snohomish Tribe

P.O. Box 1256
Port Hadlock, WA 98339
425-744-1855

> County: Jefferson
> Online: www.snohomishtribe.com
> Head of government: Chairman or chairwoman
> Legislative body: Snohomish Tribal Council
> Treaty: Treaty of Point Elliott, 1855
> Language: Lushootseed

Snoqualmoo Nation

2613 Pacific St.
Bellingham, WA 98226
360-671-1387

> County: Whatcom
> Online: www.snoqualmoonation.com
> Head of government: Chairman or chairwoman
> Legislative body: Snoqualmoo Nation Tribal Council
> Treaty: Treaty of Point Elliott, 1855
> Language: Lushootseed

Steilacoom Tribe

P.O. Box 88419
Steilacoom, WA 98388
253-584-6308

County: Pierce
Online: http://steilacoomtribe.blogspot.com
Head of government: Chairman or chairwoman
Legislative body: Steilacoom Tribal Council
Treaty: Treaty of Medicine Creek, 1854
Language: Whulshootseed

———

Those that have petitioned the U.S. government for recognition or restoration of their government-to-government relationship with the United States

Chinook Indian Nation

3 E. Park St., P.O. Box 368
Bay Center, WA 98527
360-875-6670

County: Pacific
Online: www.chinooknation.org
Head of government: Chairman or chairwoman
Legislative body: Chinook Tribal Council
Treaty: Tansy Point Treaty, 1851, never ratified by Congress;
Quinault River Treaty, 1856.
Language: Chinook

Duwamish Tribe
4705 W. Marginal Way SW
Seattle, WA 98106
206-431-1582

County: King
Online: www.duwamishtribe.org
Head of government: Chairman or chairwoman
Legislative body: Duwamish Tribal Council
Treaty: Treaty of Point Elliott, 1855
Language: Whulshootseed

---

*Those that are federally recognized, headquartered outside
Washington state, with ceded territories in Washington state*

Coeur d'Alene Tribe
850 A St.
Plummer, ID 83851
208-686-1800
Online: www.cdatribe-nsn.gov
Head of government: Chairman or chairwoman
Legislative body: Coeur d'Alene Tribal Council
Treaty: 1887 Coeur d'Alene/United States Treaty;
1889 Coeur d'Alene/United States Treaty;
1894 Coeur d'Alene/United States Treaty.
Language: Snchitsu'umshtsn

Nez Perce Tribe
P.O. Box 305
Lapwai, ID 83540
208-843-2253

Online: www.nezperce.org
Head of government: Chairman or chairwoman
Legislative body: Nez Perce Tribal Executive Committee
Treaty: Nez Perce Treaty, 1855; Nez Perce Treaty, 1863
Language: Niimiipuutímt

Confederated Tribes of the Umatilla Indian Reservation
73239 Confederated Way
Pendleton, OR 97801
541-276-3165

Online: www.ctuir.org
Head of government: Chairman or chairwoman
Legislative body: CTUIR Board of Trustees
Treaty: Treaty of Walla Walla, 1855
Language: Sahaptin

Confederated Tribes of the Warm Springs Reservation
1233 Veterans St.
Warm Springs, OR 97761
541-553-1161

Online: www.warmsprings.com
Head of government: Chairman or chairwoman
Legislative body: Warm Springs Tribal Council
Treaty: Treaty of Wasco, Columbia River, Oregon Territory, 1855
Languages: Kiksht (Wasco), Numu (Paiute), and Ichishkiin
(Sahaptin)

OTHER IMPORTANT OFFICES

Affiliated Tribes of Northwest Indians
6636 NE Sandy Blvd.
Portland, OR 97213
503-249-5770 (phone), 503-249-5773 (fax)
www.atnitribes.org

Columbia River Inter-Tribal Fish Commission
700 NE Multnomah St., No. 1200
Portland, OR 97232
503-238-0667
www.crtitfc.org

The Columbia River Inter-Tribal Fish Commission coordinates management policy and provides fisheries technical services for the Nez Perce Tribe, the Confederated Tribes of the Umatilla Indian Reservation, the Confederated Tribes of Warm Springs, and the Yakama Nation. The commission's mission is "to ensure a unified voice in the overall management of the fishery resources, and as managers, to protect reserved treaty rights through the exercise of the inherent sovereign powers of the Tribes."

Governor's Office of Indian Affairs
210 11th Ave. SW, Suite 415
P.O. Box 40909
Olympia, WA 98504-0909
360-902-8827
www.goia.wa.gov

Northwest Indian College

2522 Kwina Road
Bellingham, WA 98226
360-676-2772
www.nwic.edu

Northwest Indian Fisheries Commission

6730 Martin Way E.
Olympia, WA 98516
360-438-1180
www.nwifc.org

The NWIFC assists its member Tribes in their role as natural resources co-managers. The commission provides direct services to Tribes in areas such as biometrics, fish health and salmon management to achieve an economy of scale that makes more efficient use of limited federal funding. The NWIFC also provides a forum for Tribes to address shared natural resources management issues and enables the Tribes to speak with a unified voice in Washington, D.C.

Northwest Intertribal Court System

20818 44th Ave. West, Suite 120
Lynnwood, WA 98036
425-774-5808
www.nics.ws

Washington Indian Gaming Association

1110 Capitol Way S., Suite 404
Olympia, WA 98501
360-352-3248 (phone), 360-352-4819 (fax)
www.washingtonindiangaming.org

Washington Office of Native Education

Old Capitol Building
600 Washington St. SE
Olympia, WA 98504-7200
360-725-6160
www.k12.wa.us/IndianEd

DIRECTORY OF INDIAN COUNTRY MEDIA IN WASHINGTON STATE

*Most of these publications can be viewed online
at the Tribal government's website.*

Chehalis Confederated Tribes
Chehalis Tribal Newsletter

420 Howanut Road
Oakville, WA 98568
360-709-1726

Colville Confederated Tribes
Tribal Tribune

P.O. Box 150
Nespelem, WA 99155
888-881-7684

Hoh Tribe
Hoh Tribe Newsletter

2464 Lower Hoh Road
Forks, WA 98331
360-374-6582

Jamestown S'Klallam Tribe
News from The Strong People

1033 Old Blyn Highway
Sequim, WA 98382
360-681-3410

Kalispel Tribe
Smoke Signals

P.O. Box 39
Usk, WA 99180
509-445-1147

Lower Elwha Klallam Tribe
Elwha News

2851 Lower Elwha Road
Port Angeles, WA 98362-0298
360-452-8471

Lummi Nation
Squol Quol

2616 Kwina Road
Bellingham, WA 98226
360-384-2393

Makah Nation
Makah Tribal News

P.O. Box 115
Neah Bay, WA 98357
360-645-3286

Muckleshoot Tribe
Muckleshoot Monthly

39015 172nd Ave. SE
Auburn, WA 98002
253-939-3311

Nisqually Tribe
Nisqually Tribal News

4820 She-Nah-Num Drive SE
Olympia, WA 98513
360-456-5221

Nooksack Tribe
Snee-Nee-Chum

P.O. Box 157
Deming, WA 98244
360-592-5176

Port Gamble S'Klallam Tribe
syecem

31912 Little Boston Road NE
Kingston, WA 98346
360-297-2646

Puyallup Tribe
Puyallup Tribal News

2002 E. 28th St.
Tacoma, WA 98404
253-573-7915

Quileute Nation
The Talking Raven

P.O. Box 279
La Push, WA 98350
360-374-7760

Quinault Indian Nation
Nugguam

P.O. Box 189
Taholah, WA 98587
360-276-8211

Samish Nation
Samish News

P.O. Box 217
Anacortes, WA 98221
360-293-6404, ext. 101

Sauk-Suiattle Tribe
Sauk-Suiattle Newsletter

5318 Chief Brown Lane
Darrington, WA 98241
360-436-0131

Shoalwater Bay Tribe
Namps Chaahts

P.O. Box 130
Tokeland, WA 98590
800-633-5218, ext. 2103

Skokomish Tribe
The Sounder

80 N. Tribal Center Road
Shelton, WA 98584
360-426-4232, ext. 231

Spokane Tribe
The Rawhide Press

P.O. Box 100
Wellpinit, WA 99040
509-258-9373

Squaxin Island Tribe
Klah-Che-Min

SE 70 Squaxin Lane
Shelton, WA 98584
360-426-9781, ext. 245

Stillaguamish Tribe
Stillaguamish Tribal Newsletter

3439 Stoluckquamish Lane
Arlington, WA 98223
360-652-7362

Suquamish Tribe
Suquamish News

P.O. Box 498
Suquamish, WA 98392
360-598-3311, ext. 410

Swinomish Tribe
Qyuuqs

P.O. Box 817
LaConner, WA 98257
360-466-1732

Tulalip Tribes
See-Yat-Sub

Tulalip TV (www.kanutv.com)

NorthWest Indian News (www.nwin.com)

6729 Totem Beach Road
Marysville, WA 98270-9694
360-651-4330

Upper Skagit Tribe
Upper Skagit Newsletter

2284 Community Plaza
Sedro-Woolley, WA 98284
360-856-5501

Yakama Indian Nation
Yakama Nation Review

P.O. Box 310
Toppenish, WA 98948
509-865-5121, ext. 4717

BRIEFING ON AMERICAN INDIAN LAW

By **GABRIEL S. GALANDA**
and **AMBER PENN-ROCO**
Galanda Broadman, PLLC
www.galandabroadman.com

Tribal Sovereignty

When reporting in and around Washington Indian Country, a reporter should be aware of the concept of Tribal sovereignty.

First and foremost, Tribes are governments. Tribes compose distinct nations, each with its own political system and legal structure. Tribes are legally recognized as "distinct, independent political communities, retaining their original natural rights" in matters of local self-government. *Worcester v. Georgia*, 31 U.S. 515, 559 (1832).

Tribes remain a "separate people, with the power of regulating their internal and social relations." *U.S. v. Kagama*, 118 U.S. 375, 381–82 (1886). As such, Tribes enjoy the inherent right to "make their own laws and be ruled by them." *Williams v. Lee*, 358 U.S. 217, 220 (1959).

In summary, Tribal sovereignty is the inherent authority of a Tribe to create its own laws and govern itself and its relations in Indian Country. *Id.* Conversely, state law generally "can have no force" in Indian Country. *Worcester*, 31 U.S. at 561.

A Tribe's inherent sovereignty is likely affirmed by a treaty with the United States, which the federal constitution recognizes as the "supreme law of the land" (U.S. Const., Art. VI, cl. 2.); or a presidential executive order, which is generally of the "same legal ramifications" as a treaty. *Timpanogos Tribe v. Conway*, 286 F.3d 1195, 1202, n.3 (10th Cir. 2002).

For a reporter, beyond appreciating the existence of a Tribe's treaty or executive order, it is key to understand that each Tribe has its own unique set of laws and protocols that must be respected. These Tribal laws, which are written, codified or published, or unwritten, uncodified or unpublished, can concern a wide variety of topics that may impact a reporter, including rights of land access and cultural property protection (i.e., laws concerning rights to art, dances and songs). When dealing with a Tribe, it is critical to remember that not every Tribe is the same; it should be recognized that your interactions with Tribes may differ based on the individual practices of that Tribe.

Inquiry must be made about applicable Tribal law prior to, or alternatively at the very outset of, any interaction with a Tribe or entry upon Tribal lands. In particular, a reporter should immediately seek Tribal permission to inquire of the Tribe or enter Tribal lands, as discussed below.

Tribal Governance

A Tribe's sovereignty and laws are typically implemented by an executive authority such as a Tribal chairperson (similar to the U.S. president or a state's governor) and a Tribal council or senate (the legislative body). Tribal courts adjudicate most matters arising from a Tribe's territories or under Tribal law. But for traditional reasons, Tribes do not necessarily follow an Anglo-American constitutional model of separation of powers.

A reporter should primarily appreciate that his or her interface with the Tribe may initially, or primarily, be with the Tribe's figurehead or his or her staff, although permission to do anything within the Tribe's territories may require Tribal legislative action.

Tribal Sovereign Immunity

Like the United States and state governments, Tribal governments are generally immune from suit. In general, a Tribe or any of its parts may only be sued if Congress has "unequivocally" authorized the suit or the Tribe has "clearly" waived Tribal sovereign immunity. *Kiowa Tribe v. Manufacturing Technologies*, 523 U.S. 757 (1998). Tribal immunity generally extends to Tribal officials and employees in their official capacity and Tribal agencies and businesses, whether within or beyond the boundaries of the Tribe's reservation.

For reporting purposes, Tribal immunity shields Tribal governments from lawsuits or third-party subpoenas for information. In addition, few, if any, Tribal governments have public records laws. Therefore, a reporter seeking information in the possession of a Tribe can likely only obtain documents or other information through a polite request.

Tribal Jurisdiction

Tribal authority typically hinges upon the classification and ownership of Indian or reservation land – or more specifically, what is considered "Indian Country." Indian Country is a federal statutory term that includes all land within the exterior boundaries of Indian reservations, as well as dependent Indian communities, and Indian allotments for which the Indian titles have not been extinguished. 18 USC 1151. There are generally two categories of land title in Indian Country: (1) trust land, and (2) non-trust land. Trust land is land that is held by the federal government. Trust land may be controlled by the Tribe or may be individual allotments held by Tribal members. Non-trust (or fee) land may be held by Tribes, Tribal members or nonmembers.

Indian Tribes have regulatory authority over Tribal members and nonmembers on Indian Country land. *Washington v. Confederated Tribes of the Colville Indian Reservation*, 447 U.S. 134 (1980). Within the boundaries of reservations, and on trust lands, Tribes can regulate like any other government. *Atkinson Trading Post v. Shirley*, 532 U.S. 645 (2001). While a 1953 federal law known as "Public Law 280" or "PL-280," and its Washington State counterpart of the same namesake, has made some state laws applicable on Indian lands in Washington, the assertion of state jurisdiction is generally considered to be concurrent with Tribal authority. RCW 27.12; Vanessa J. Jimenez & Soo C. Song, *Concurrent Tribal and State Jurisdiction Under Public Law 280*, 47 AM. U. L. REV. 1627 (1998).

In general, Tribes can only assert jurisdiction over non-Indians in Indian Country if the non-Indian has entered into a consensual relationship with the Tribe or its members (typically a contract or lease); or partaken in conduct that threatens or has some direct effect on the political integrity, economic security, or health and welfare of the Tribe. *Montana v. U.S.*, 450 U.S. 544 (1981). However, nonmembers living, working or doing business on Indian Country lands are generally subject to the jurisdiction of the Tribe whose lands they enter or occupy. *Water Wheel Camp Recreational Area, Inc. v. LaRance*, 642 F.3d 802 (9th Cir. 2011).

In general, a reporter should be aware that a Tribe likely has authority over his or her own conduct and his or her employer's conduct in Indian Country.

Right to Exclude

While reporters may believe they have legal access to any place usually considered "public," this is not the case on reservations. As a part of a Tribe's inherent sovereignty, a Tribe has a right to exclude nonmembers from entering Tribal lands.

This inherent right to exclude was first affirmed in 1821, in a U.S. Attorney General opinion. "So long as a tribe exist and remains in possession of its lands, its title and possession are sovereign and exclusive; and there exists no authority to enter upon their lands, for any purpose whatever, without their consent." 1 U.S. Op. Atty. Gen. 465, 465 (Apr. 26, 1821). This inherent right remains intact today. *See Water Wheel Camp Recreational Area, Inc. v. LaRance*, 642 F.3d 802 (9th Cir. 2011).

Before a reporter enters a reservation or any Indian Country, he or she should first consult with the Tribal authority. A Tribe may choose to grant access, deny access, or grant access with conditions. By consulting with a Tribe prior to entering Tribal grounds, a reporter demonstrates respect for the Tribe's authority and a reporter may avoid subsequent disputes over access.

As a reporter becomes familiar with practicing in Indian Country, the complexity surrounding interactions with a Tribe will become more apparent. Overall, it is important to remember that a Tribe's sovereignty means that a reporter is dealing with a distinct entity, whose own laws and practices should be respected in order to develop a good relationship with the Tribe and establish a trustworthy reputation within the community.

– Gabriel S. Galanda is a citizen of the Round Valley Indian Tribes, and Amber-Penn Roco is a citizen of the Chehalis Tribe. They are lawyers who practice in Seattle at Galanda Broadman, PLLC, an American Indian-owned law firm specializing in American Indian law.

BRIEFING ON NEWS GATHERING IN INDIAN COUNTRY

By JACKIE JACOBS
*Communications specialist
and media strategist*

Sovereignty gives each of the 29 Tribes in Washington State the freedom to decide their level of contact with the press. It is important to know that they each have to be treated individually. They are not one entity, but rather individual governments that have their own rules, regulations, processes and procedures for access to information. You must contact each Tribal government to request those guidelines and permissions.

Access to Government Meetings and Records

Washington State open meetings laws do not apply to Tribal governments and access to Tribal meetings can be denied with no repercussions.

Request for Information

Reporters need to request permission for access to any information they are seeking and to cover a story on Tribal lands. The federal Freedom of Information Act (FOIA) or Washington State public records act does not apply to Tribal governments or agencies. Instead, Tribal information laws, if any, govern the dissemination of information from Tribes or on Tribal lands.

Caveat: In *Confederated Tribes of the Chehalis Reservation v. Johnson,* the Washington State Supreme Court decided in 1998 that information about Indian-run gaming was not protected by the Washington State Public Records Act when in the possession of the state. As Washington's highest court reasoned:

> The information does not, as the Tribes suggest, deal solely with the conduct of the Tribal government with no relation to state governmental processes. The Gambling Commission negotiates, renegotiates and enforces the compacts on behalf of the citizens of Washington. Also, it is involved in distributing the community contributions to governmental agencies which are affected by the Tribes' gambling operations. In order to fulfill its obligations in this regard, the Gambling Commission must rely on and use the information contained in the report requested. The records relate to the conduct of the Gambling Commission and to its governmental functions. Therefore, the records are 'public record' within the scope of the Public Records Act. 958 P.2d 260, 266 (Wash. 1998).

The same generally holds true for Tribal information in the possession of the United States, in relation to FOIA, according to a U.S. Supreme Court decision. *Department of the Interior v. Klamath Water Users Protection Assn.,* 532 U.S. 1 (2001).

However, these rulings have caused Tribes to recoil from sharing sensitive information from state of federal government so most often, the Tribes remain the best sources of information.

Deadlines

Reporters should be aware that some requests for permission will need to be presented to the Tribal Council for consideration and/or approval. In those instances, please be aware that a response could take between 1-3 weeks. This information is intended to provide insight so you can meet your deadlines.

Etiquette in Indian Country

Each Tribe makes decisions on how best to balance community and tradition. In an effort to avoid misunderstandings or violations of their customs, visitors are asked to follow basic procedures for conduct. This is necessary to protect sacred and ceremonial areas, including the preservation of historical artifacts.

- Please be attentive to signage, and obey individual Tribal rules and regulations.

- Please respect the privacy of residential communities.

- Request permission in advance prior to photographing or recording an individual, an event, and/or an activity.

- Do not pick up or remove artifacts or objects, such as beach driftwood, broken pottery, eagle feathers, marine growth, minerals, rocks, sand, shells, etc. Each Tribe has ordinances for prevention and protection of their natural resources.

- Burial grounds are sacred sites and are protected by U.S. federal law.

- Religious ceremonies are sacred and are not to be entered without prior permission or invitation.

Native Americans are hospitable and generous by nature. However, spiritual teachings, sacred ceremonies and burial grounds are not openly shared with the public.

– Jackie Jacobs is owner of Medicine Wheel Media-Public Relations and Marketing, a division of JTalentgroup in Seattle. She is a citizen of the Lumbee Tribe.

NOTES

NOTES

NOTES

NOTES

NOTES

NOTES

www.ingramcontent.com/pod-product-compliance
Lightning Source LLC
Chambersburg PA
CBHW071246020426
42333CB00015B/1651